# Pocket Mandalas Coloring Book

# Pocket Mandalas Coloring Book

Mini Zen Creations for Portable Relaxation and Mindfulness

mage Credits: All images are sourced from Shutterstock.com. Cover image © Snezh. ack cover images © Snezh, © il67. Interior images © Snezh except for: page 11 © Iagnia; page 19 © Yaviki; page 27 © Kotkoa; page 35 © New Line; pages 39, 81, 87, 5 © CkyBe; page 41 © Real Illusion; page 43 © il67; pages 51, 59, 67, 75, 83, 91 © unarus; page 69 © karakotsya; page 79 © De-v

rinted by: Createspace.com

0 9 8 7 6 5 4 3 2 1

Iay, 2015
Jew York, New York, USA

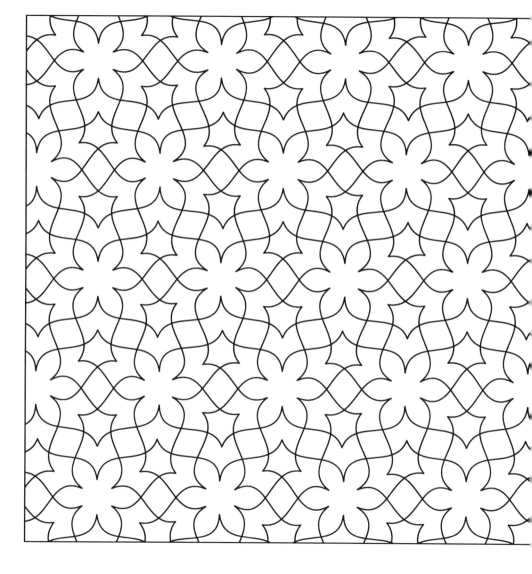

26530438R00055

Made in the USA
Middletown, DE
01 December 2015